BLACK HOLES

ENERGY

GALAXIES

GRAVITY

LIGHT

MYSTERIES OF
THE UNIVERSE

MASS & MATTER

SPACE & TIME

STARS

MYSTERIES OF THE UNIVERSE

Gravity

JIM WHITING

CREATIVE EDUCATION

Published by Creative Education
P.O. Box 227, Mankato, Minnesota 56002
Creative Education is an imprint of The Creative Company
www.thecreativecompany.us

Design and production by Blue Design
Art direction by Rita Marshall
Printed in the United States of America

Photographs by European Space Agency, Getty Images (AFP, Central Press,
Norman Cooper, Hulton Archive, Polish School, SSPL, Universal History
Archive, Visuals Unlimited, Inc./Carol & Mike Werner), iStockphoto
(Warwick Lister-Kaye, Rafael Ramirez Lee, Alexey Shchepetilnikov, Tony
Tremblay), NASA (NASA, NASA/CXC/MIT/C. Canizares/M. Nowak/
NASA/STScl, NASA/ESA/Hubble Heritage Team, NASA/ESA/K. Sharon [Tel
Aviv University]/E. Ofek [Caltech], NASA/JPL, NASA/JPL/Space Science
Institute, NASA/Paul Riedel/Al Lukas)

Cover and folio illustration © 2011 Alex Ryan

Library of Congress Cataloging-in-Publication Data
Whiting, Jim.
Gravity / by Jim Whiting.
p. cm. — (Mysteries of the universe)
Includes bibliographical references and index.
Summary: An examination of the science behind the physical phenomenon
known as gravity, including relevant theories and history-making
discoveries as well as topics of current and future research.
ISBN 978-1-60818-189-6
1. Gravity—Juvenile literature. I. Title.

QC178.W46 2012
531'.14—dc23   2011040142

First Edition
9 8 7 6 5 4 3 2 1

The sport of weightlifting depends upon gravity

TABLE OF CONTENTS

Gravity is at work everywhere, even amidst Saturn's rings

INTRODUCTION

For most of human history, the true nature of the universe was shrouded in myth and mystery. About 400 years ago, scientists began unraveling those mysteries. Their efforts were so successful that American **physicist** Albert Michelson wrote in 1894, "The more important fundamental laws and facts of physical science have all been discovered, and these are now so firmly established that the possibility of their ever being supplemented in consequence of new discoveries is exceedingly remote." William Thomson, Baron Kelvin, perhaps that era's most famous physicist, echoed Michelson: "There is nothing new to be discovered in physics now. All that remains is more and more precise measurement." Both men were wrong. Within a few years, scientists had revealed the makeup of the tiny **atom** and the unexpected vastness of outer space. Yet the universe doesn't yield its mysteries easily, and much remains to be discovered.

Gravity is one of those areas in which further discoveries await scientists. The effects of gravity are easily observable. Things fall down, not up. People don't float off into the sky. Because of gravity, everything weighs a certain number of pounds (or kilograms)—unless they venture into outer space, in which case they are weightless. Scientists have a pretty good idea about how gravity works, and they can even measure how strong it is. But they really have no idea *why* it works, especially on Earth, where its force seems just right. That is gravity's enduring mystery.

Baron Kelvin worked mainly in energy-related areas of physics

INTRODUCTION

GOING UP AND COMING DOWN

What goes up must come down. This obvious—and seemingly simple—statement masks one of the most complex forces in the entire universe. That force is gravity. Without it, the universe would be completely chaotic. Virtually everything, from a child jumping up and down to the motion of the stars through the heavens, depends on gravity. Indirectly, it even determines the length of the week and the names of its seven days. Despite more than three centuries of study, scientists still don't completely understand this essential force.

Gravity is one of the four fundamental forces of nature recognized by scientists. These forces act upon matter in different ways and with vastly different strengths. The most powerful force is the strong nuclear force, which binds the **protons** and **neutrons** in the nucleus, or center, of an atom. Because the positive electrical charge of protons would normally repel them from each other, it requires a great deal of force to overcome this repulsion.

The strong nuclear force is 100 times stronger than the electromagnetic force. Electromagnetism consists of a series of waves of different lengths and involves matter or energy that carries an electric charge. This force can attract or repel objects. Magnets, microwaves, **radio waves**, and visible light are all examples of the electromagnetic force at work.

The third fundamental force is the weak nuclear force. It is responsible for **radioactive** decay in atoms, resulting in reactions that not only aid in the generation of sunlight but also provide the means for certain types of medical diagnoses and treatment and help researchers such as **archaeologists** and **geologists** determine the age of the objects they are studying.

Gravity is the weakest of the four fundamental forces. It is no match for electromagnetism. For example, if you hold a magnet over a nail, the nail will instantly rise and attach itself to the magnet. Airplanes also defy gravity. A fully loaded 747 jetliner, for example, can weigh up to 870,000 pounds (394,625 kg). Yet from a dead stop, this

Gravity brings a jumping child back
to a trampoline's surface

An airplane counteracts gravity with the help of other forces

massive aircraft becomes airborne in less than a minute as it roars down the runway. That's because the **lift** from its wings and the **thrust** from its engines overcome the downward pull of gravity. As long as the airplane has enough fuel to power its engines, it will stay in the air. Even a person bending over to pick up a stick of wood represents a small victory over gravity.

Gravity is what enables us to enjoy thrill rides in amusement parks. For example, roller coasters are pulled high up, then gravity takes over as they hurtle downward. For added thrills, many people flock to loop-the-loop rides, in which you are upside down for a brief moment at the top of the loop. Although you're strapped in for safety, you wouldn't fall, even if you weren't restrained. That's because the acceleration that pushes you against the back of your seat cancels out the pull of gravity. In fact, you might actually feel a little lighter than usual.

How much everything weighs is also determined by gravity. We may not be physically aware of it, but gravity actually pushes down on us with a force of 32.2 feet (9.8 m) per second. Because we spend most of our lives in contact with something that keeps us from falling toward the center of the earth, we don't notice the strength of this force. The moment a swimmer steps off a diving board or a skydiver leaps from an airplane, however, the pull of gravity becomes apparent as the person hurtles downward.

This pull of gravity isn't the same everywhere. A person who weighs 150 pounds (68 kg) on Earth would weigh just 25 pounds (11.3 kg) on the moon because Earth is bigger than the moon, and its gravity is stronger. That same person would weigh 354 pounds (160.6 kg) on Jupiter because that planet is even larger than Earth.

It's important to realize that weight is not the same as mass. Mass refers to the amount of matter that any object—whether living or not—contains. A lineman on a professional football team has much more mass than a baby, and because of this, the force of gravity on him is considerably greater. Therefore, he weighs more. If both the

lineman and the baby were to find themselves high above Earth in space, they would continue to have the same mass. But the downward pull of gravity on them would no longer exist, so neither one would weigh anything.

The weightlessness of people in space illustrates another aspect of gravity. Television viewers might laugh at the antics of astronauts who seem to float in space vehicles. But there's a serious side to weightlessness. Astronauts can lose up to five percent of their muscle mass in a short time in conditions of weightlessness. Bone **density** can also decrease. Some astronauts become so weak that they have to be carried off in stretchers when they return to Earth. That's because gravity is essential for the growth of muscles and their continued health. Whether people lift weights, run, or swim, muscle development comes from pushing back against the force of gravity. To overcome the negative effects of weightlessness, astronauts—especially those who spend months aboard the **International Space Station**—exercise while they are in space. According to Don Hagan, director of exercise physiology at the Johnson Space Center in Houston, Texas, "No other activity except eating and sleeping is given that much priority. Two and a half hours each day are devoted to fitness."

Sometimes it can be beneficial to reduce the effects of gravity while exercising. For example, injured athletes may train in water because a person weighs less in water than he or she does on dry land. Some people have even trained for marathons by doing only pool running. The water absorbs most of the force of each stride, so their muscles and joints aren't as stressed and are able to recover more quickly. Water therapy can also be advantageous for animals such as dogs and racehorses. One horse suffered a significant leg injury six weeks before a major competition and underwent daily pool sessions. The horse ended up winning a bronze medal.

All objects, regardless of size, exert a pull of gravity on all other objects. If you and a

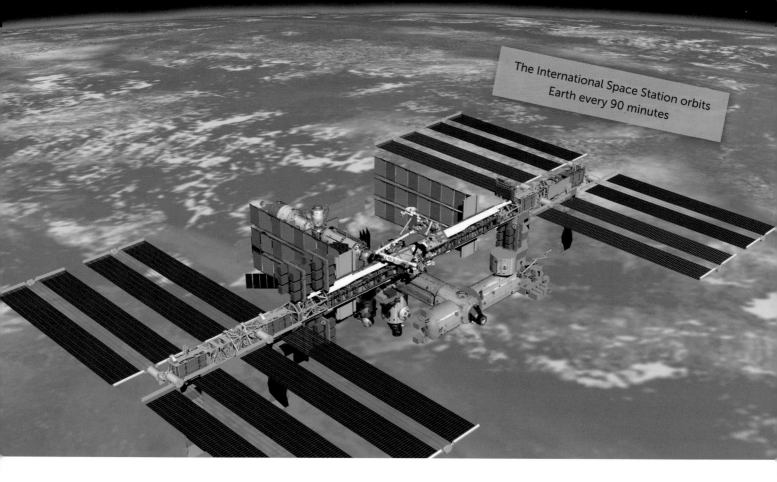

friend stand a few feet apart, there is a tiny gravitational attraction between the two of you. But the actual effect of your bodies on each other is so minuscule that it doesn't make any difference in your interaction.

When it comes to huge celestial bodies, on the other hand, gravity makes a big difference. The pull of the sun is so strong that Earth and the other planets remain in **orbit** around it, while the moon orbits Earth. As the moon circles Earth, its gravitational pull moves the water in the oceans toward it by a few feet, while Earth's gravity pulls away from the water. As Earth continues to spin, these changes in water levels begin to subside, and the tide goes down.

One tidal cycle lasts a little more than 12 hours, as the moon also moves partway around Earth—about 6 degrees—in that time. Because the positions of Earth, the sun, and the moon can be determined by mathematical formulas, tides are predicted months ahead. From natural forces to human creations, gravity influences everything on Earth. And its influence doesn't stop here. It extends far beyond Earth, all the way to the edge of the universe.

GOING UP AND COMING DOWN

Gravity brings water crashing down from Argentina's Iguazú Falls

16

THE FORCE THAT'S WITH US

Since humans appeared on Earth, the force of gravity has always been observable. If early people picked something up and dropped it, the object always fell to the ground. If they tripped, they fell flat on their face. If they jumped, they came back down. They saw that water flowed downhill, not uphill. They realized that hiking up a steep hill was harder than walking on level ground. And they took it for granted that they would remain anchored to the ground as they went about their daily business, rather than floating off into the sky.

But no one knew why these things happened. About 2,500 years ago, the ancient Greeks began trying to figure out the reasons. The most famous of these Greeks was the philosopher Aristotle, who developed theories about the natural world that dominated the way people thought for nearly 2,000 years. For instance, Aristotle believed that the more an object weighed, the faster it would fall. That seemed only natural. So natural, in fact, that he didn't bother to check his facts. As modern British physicist Stephen Hawking has observed, Aristotle thought "one could work out all the laws that govern the universe by pure thought: it was not necessary to check by observation."

Many Greek philosophers such as Aristotle believed that the most perfect geometric form was the circle. So they thought the universe consisted of a series of concentric spheres, with Earth at the center of this system. The moon was in the first sphere from Earth, while the sun and other planets were placed in successive spheres farther away. This model is known as the geocentric, or Earth-centered, universe. Aristotle also believed that everything on Earth was made up of four basic elements: earth (the heaviest), water, air, and fire (the lightest). Each element had its own concentric sphere, and motion was the result of elements seeking out their natural sphere. Objects composed primarily of fire would float upward. Objects made primarily of earth would fall. They would stop falling when they encountered something solid, such as the dirt or stones of Earth's surface.

Like the Greeks, other ancient peoples such as the Egyptians and **Babylonians** turned their attention to the heavens and made systematic studies. They discovered that the sun, moon, and stars followed predictable paths. Regarding the sun and moon, such predictability had a practical benefit, as the ancients constructed calendars based on the regular movements of these two bodies. Yet early **astronomers** soon discovered there was a flaw in their concept of an orderly universe. Five mysterious "stars" didn't behave like the others. Sometimes they even appeared to move backwards. The Greeks called them *planetai*—which means "wandering"—the source of our word "planet." Along with the sun and moon, these five planets (Mercury, Venus, Mars, Jupiter, and Saturn) took on so much importance in the eyes of their discoverers that they became objects of worship.

No one in the ancient world saw any

36TH. DEKAN. HERT-REMEN-SAHU (CHILDREN OF HORUS)

AMENOPHIS (III) HER BELOVED

ISIS-SIRIUS

& STRENGTH LIKE THE SUN

PHARAOH

33RD & 34TH DEKANS SAHU = ORION

32ND. DEKAN. KHERT - SAHU (OSIRIS)

35TH. DEKAN (EYE OF HORUS)

31ST. DEKAN. KHERT-REMEN SAHU (CHILDREN OF HORUS)

MAAT-NEB-RÈ TITLE OF PHARAOH

30TH. DEKAN. KHAU, & BODY) (CHILDREN OF HORUS & BODY)

28TH. & 29TH DEKANS, KOD & SASAKOD (HAPI & KEBHSNUF)

26TH. & 27TH. DEKANS. KHENT-HER & KHER (THE CHILDREN OF HORUS)

25TH. DEKAN. BAIU. (HAPI)

24TH. DEKAN. KHU-U. (TUAMUTEF)

23RD. DEKAN. TEPAKHU. (TUA-ATEF)

22ND DEKAN. KHER-KEPD-SERT (KEBH-SNUF)

21ST. DEKAN. SASA-SÀT (TUAMUTEF)

20TH. DEKAN. SÀT (BODY OF ISIS)

18TH. DEKAN. TEPA-

17TH. DEKAN. KO

16TH. DEKAN.

15TH. DEK

14TH.

DEKAN. SMAD (AMSET)

THE BOAT OF SIRIUS

THE BOAT OF ORION

JUPITER

GREAT BEAR

BOOTES

(TAURUS) (ARIES) THE "BODY"

THE RAM (AQUILA) (THE MILKY WAY)

THE SUN BOAT (SCORPIO)

ARMAYA

THE CIRCUMPOLAR STARS

ISIS (S) (FOR AMSET)

HAPI (N) (TUAMUTEF)

THE CHILDREN OF HORUS

KEBHSNUF (W)

MAAENTEF

THE GRANDCHILDREN OF HORUS

GENII

(PROBABLY PRAYER FOR PHARAOH HERE)

PTAH GOD OF PHARAOH THE IIND. MONTH

TEKHI GODDESS OF THE IST. MONTH

BABOON; ORIFICE OF CLEPSYDRA

HARMACHIS GOD OF THE XIITH MONTH

APET GODDESS OF THE XITH MONTH

PRAYERS FOR PHARAOH

HORUS KHENTI-KHAT GOD OF THE XTH MONTH

KHONSU GOD OF THE IXTH MONTH

PRAYERS FOR PHARAOH

RENUNET GODDESS OF THE VIIITH MONTH

ROSAU. NETCHED JACKAL GOD OF THE VIITH MONTH

GOD (PHARAOH)

HOR PRAYERS FOR PHARAOH

THE KARNAK CLEPSYDRA

[AMENOPHIS III : CIRCA 1400 B.C]

CELESTIAL DIAGRAM ON EXTERIOR SURFACE

SMALL RESTORATIONS, FROM CEILINGS OF TOMB OF SENMUT [1500 B.C] & RAMESSEUM [1300 B.C]

19

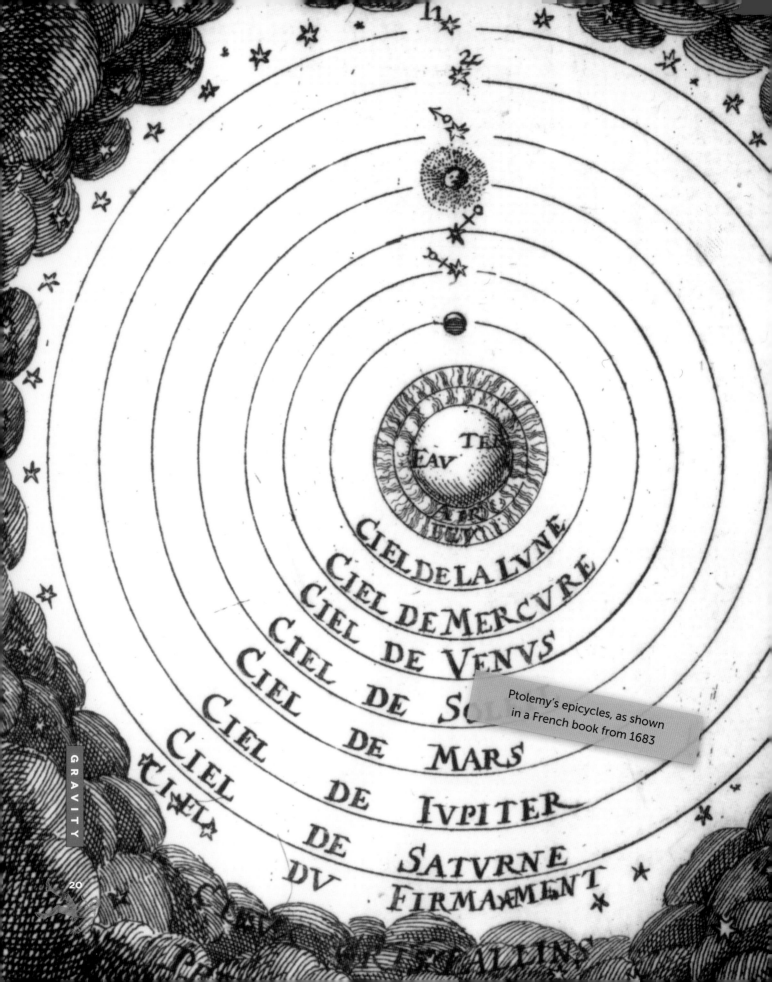

CIEL DE LA LVNE
CIEL DE MERCVRE
CIEL DE VENVS
CIEL DE SO[...]
CIEL DE MARS
CIEL DE IVPITER
CIEL DE SATVRNE
CIEL DV FIRMAMENT

TE[...]
EAV

Ptolemy's epicycles, as shown in a French book from 1683

GRAVITATIONAL ASIDES

Giraffes in Space?

The first appearance of giraffes in Paris, France, in 1827 created a sensation. Women piled their hair high to imitate the animal's long neck, and men wore extra-tall "giraffique" hats. More than 150 years later, giraffes inspired another fashion: tight-fitting "gravity suits" for astronauts. Scientists studied giraffes to see how they overcame gravity by pumping blood all the way up their long necks to their heads. They also wondered why giraffes didn't faint when they lowered their heads to drink and then quickly raised them again. According to the laws of gravity, the blood should have rushed down their long neck veins and pooled in their legs and feet. Scientists then discovered that giraffes have some of the largest hearts in the animal kingdom. These bigger hearts are more effective at pumping blood to giraffes' extremities. Giraffes also have one-way valves in their neck veins that keep the blood from rushing downward. Another gravity-defying factor is the animals' tight skin, which maintains enough pressure on the veins in their legs that blood is able to circulate with greater ease. Space researchers studied this skin as they developed gravity suits for astronauts. These suits work in much the same way, helping an astronaut maintain a constant blood pressure in his or her body while experiencing weightlessness.

connection between movements high in the sky and people's everyday experiences on Earth, though. Everyone who subscribed to Aristotle's view believed the heavenly bodies were embedded in unvarying spheres, incapable of change. Aristotle thought these bodies must be made of a different element, **ether**, which was separate from the four earthly ones. Thus the way things happened on Earth and the way things happened in the heavens were subject to two entirely different sets of laws.

n the second century A.D., the Greek-born astronomer Claudius Ptolemy combined all the observations of his predecessors in one unified theory. To account for the erratic motions of the planets, he developed a complicated system of epicycles, or circles within existing circles, and assigned celestial bodies to these different positions. His book the *Almagest* (*The Great Compilation*), written around A.D. 150, served as the primary astronomy text for more than 1,400 years as people continued to believe in a geocentric universe.

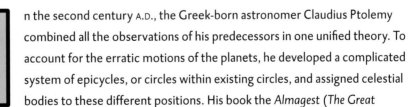

The telescope of 17th-century Polish astronomer Johannes Hevelius

Things began to change in the 1500s. Based on further observations, scientists and mathematicians began proposing theories suggesting that Earth wasn't at the center of the universe. They argued that everything revolved around the sun instead. This theory was called heliocentrism, from the Greek word *helios*, or "sun."

The invention of the telescope in the early 1600s helped advance the heliocentric theory. Now that people could see the heavens more closely, it became apparent that the universe wasn't geocentric. The competition between the two theories finally ended in the 17th century with English scientist Isaac Newton's discovery that the same force—gravity—that held things together on Earth was also the "glue" that maintained order and balance in the heavens. It was even possible to measure the strength of this force. As contemporary American mathematician Joseph Mazur observes about that time in his book *The Motion Paradox: The 2,500-Year-Old Puzzle behind All the Mysteries of Time and Space*, "Suddenly the entire universe is filled with bodies, large and small, pulling each other in all directions, everything pulling everything, apples pulling planets, planets pulling apples." It was a startling revelation.

ncreased knowledge of gravity helped astronomers learn more about the mysteries of the heavens. After the planet Uranus was discovered in 1781, astronomers realized that the orbit they had predicted for it didn't match its actual orbit. In 1846, French mathematician Urbain Jean Joseph Le Verrier theorized that an unknown planet was the cause of this discrepancy and calculated where he thought it should be. He contacted Germany's Berlin Observatory, which turned its telescopes to Le Verrier's predicted position and spotted the planet immediately. The planet was named Neptune.

People soon began to wonder if it would be possible to escape gravity's effects and soar into the heavens. Near the end of the 19th century, authors such as H. G. Wells and Jules Verne wrote novels about leaving Earth behind and traveling toward distant worlds. Although the works were **science fiction**, many of the innovations they described were grounded in scientific fact and even anticipated future developments.

The idea of space travel moved beyond fiction toward reality when scientists began experimenting with rockets early in the 20th century. Because of the downward pull of gravity, rockets need to go fast—very fast. The speed they must attain to soar beyond Earth is called escape velocity, which is 7 miles (11.3 km) per second, or about 25,200 miles (40,555 km) per hour. During World War II (1939–45), German scientists began making breakthroughs with the invention of powerful rockets called V-2s. Although they didn't achieve escape velocity, V-2s did soar dozens of miles upward before returning to

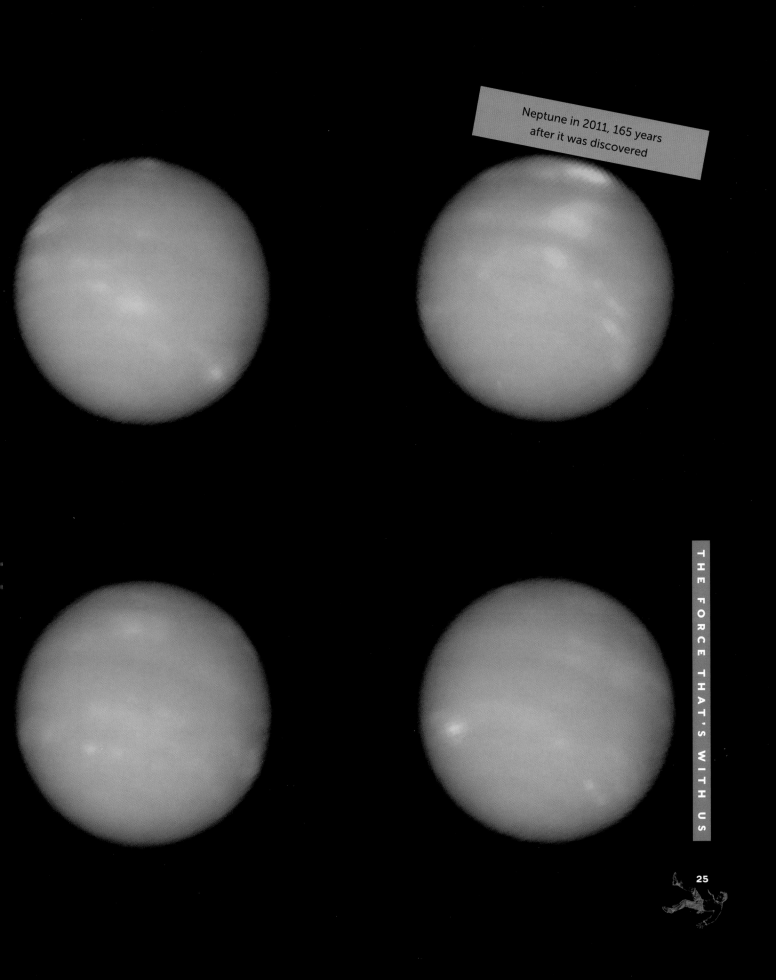

Neptune in 2011, 165 years after it was discovered

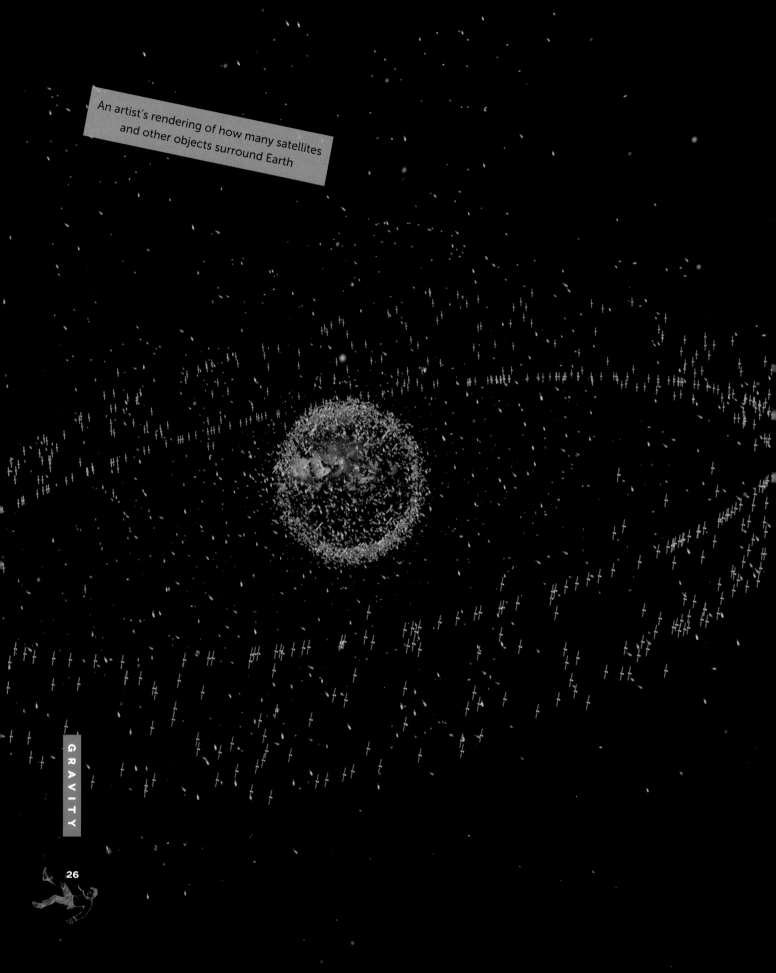

An artist's rendering of how many satellites and other objects surround Earth

GRAVITATIONAL ASIDES

Fly Me to the Moon

Perhaps the first person to write about achieving escape velocity and traveling beyond Earth was French novelist Jules Verne in his 1865 book, *From the Earth to the Moon*. Writing nearly a century before the United States' Apollo moon landing program, Verne conducted extensive research before deciding that a huge cannon with a barrel hundreds of feet long would provide enough force to blast his spacecraft to the moon. His fictional treatment shared many similarities with the real-life Apollo program. The spacecraft were both about nine feet (2.7 m) in diameter and took off from Florida. Adjusting for the changes in a dollar's value in the different eras, the costs were even similar. Verne's spacecraft was named *Columbiad*, while the Apollo command module was *Columbia*. There were significant scientific problems with Verne's story, however. Calculations soon proved that Verne's cannon would had to have been much longer than he thought. The more fundamental issue was that the pressure generated by the tremendous acceleration of *Columbiad* would have caused it to burn up within moments of being launched. Verne also wrote books about traveling to the center of the earth and the bottom of the ocean. Many consider him to be the father of science fiction.

Earth and raining death and destruction on their targets.

After the war ended, rocket research accelerated rapidly. In 1957, the Soviet Union launched a rocket carrying a basketball-sized **artificial satellite** called *Sputnik 1* into orbit around Earth. But *Sputnik* hadn't gone high enough to completely escape the pull of gravity. Within a few months, it fell out of its orbit and burned up in Earth's atmosphere.

Today, hundreds of artificial satellites orbit Earth. These satellites have uses that no one could have imagined a few decades ago. They make cell phone communication possible. They transmit television signals instantly to virtually every spot on Earth. They help forecast the weather. Satellite-mounted cameras provide crystal-clear images of our world. In recent years, Global Positioning System (GPS) satellites have helped people navigate their way down the block or around the world. And all these innovations depend on gravity.

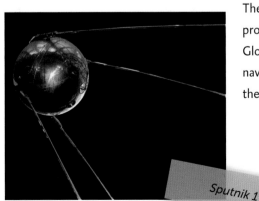

Sputnik 1

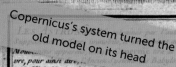
Copernicus's system turned the old model on its head

SYSTÊME DE COPERNIC.

La [...] d'Aristote [...] tous les [...] qui revivre, pour ainsi dire, [...] l'Unique et le Véritable Systême du Monde [...] à Thorn dans la Prusse Polonoise l'An 1472, et embrasa [...] astique à la sollicitation de l'Evêque de Warmie, son Oncle Maternel. Livré par goût à l'étude de l'Astronomie, il ne tarda pas longtems à reconnoître les inconveniens du Systême reçu, et l'impossibilité où l'on étoit de rendre raison, dans cette supposition, de quantité d'apparences, principalement de celle de Mercure et de Vénus. Ce qui l'engagea à proposer son Systême, est, qu'après avoir réfléchi sur la nature de ces deux Planètes, il les trouva d'une matière dense, ténébreuse et semblable à la Terre, il reconnoit qu'il aisément qu'il n'étoit pas plus difficile à la Terre de tourner autour du Soleil, que d'y voir tourner les autres Planètes. Cette Hypothèse lui parût d'autant plus naturelle, que par là il rendoit aisément raison de tous les Phénomènes. Son Opinion avoit été ébauchée par les Pythagoriciens 300 ans avant l'Ere Vulgaire, entr'autres par Aristarque Samien, par Thalès, par Anaximandre, par Anaxagore, et par plusieurs autres Philosophes : mais ils ne la soutenoient pas tous de même.

La Terre, selon quelques-uns, étoit à la Vérité, au Centre du Monde ; mais elle tournoit sur son Axe d'Orient en Occident, et montroit successivement ses parties au Soleil pour en être éclairée. Le Soleil et les Etoiles fixes avoient ce Mouvement périodique qu'ils leur croyoient propre. Cette Opinion a été renouvellée par quelques Modernes.

Le Soleil, suivant les autres, étoit au Centre de l'univers pour en éclairer et échauffer toutes les Parties, et la Terre étoit placée parmi les Planètes, à peu près où les premiers mettoient le Soleil. Le Cardinal Cusa est le premier des Modernes qui ait renouvellé ce Systême ; mais Copernic est le premier qui en ait fait un Corps de Doctrine lié et suivi. Il mourut en 1543, le jour même qu'on lui apporta le premier exemplaire de son Ouvrage. S'il eût survécu quelque tems, il auroit eu la Satisfaction de voir son Assertion regardée comme la plus vraisemblable ; Ce n'est cependant que plusieurs années après, que la Découverte du Télescope, nous en a fourni des preuves incontestables.

Le Soleil, suivant ce Systême, est placé au centre du Monde, pour répandre de tous côtés l'action et la fécondité de ses rayons. Il est le Centre des Orbites de Six Corps Sphériques et Opaques qui tournent d'Occident en Orient, Sçavoir : Mercure, qui est le plus proche du Soleil, et qui fait sa révolution en trois Mois ; Vient ensuite Vénus, dont l'Orbite est un peu plus grand, qui employe 8 mois ou environ à faire sa révolution. Plus loin est la Terre qui achève sa révolution dans l'espace de 365 jours 5 heures 49 min. Au dessus de la Terre est Mars dont la Période est de 2 ans ; mais Jupiter qui est beaucoup plus éloigné est 12 ans à faire chaque révolution. Enfin Saturne est de toutes les Planètes celle qui met le plus de tems à parcourir son Cercle autour du Soleil. Et comme son Orbite renferme toutes les autres, sa révolution périodique est de 30 ans. Au dessus de Saturne est le Firmament, ou le Ciel des Etoiles fixes qui est immobile Ces Planètes, seules, sont chargées de tout le Mouvement : Car cette apparence de mouvement rétrograde presqu'insensible, par laquel les Etoiles paroissent changer peu à peu de Déclinaison, et avancer d'un dégré en 70 ans, ne provient que de ce que la Terre, en revenant au bout d'un an, par son Mouvement, au point de l'Equinoxe du Printems, ne coupe pas justement la ligne Equinoxiale au même endroit où elle l'avoit coupée l'année précédente ; Mais un peu en deçà, de sorte qu'en 70 ans un dégré se trouve anticipé, C'est ce qu'on appelle la Précession des Equinoxes ; et le premier point du Bélier dans le Zodiaque, s'éloigne toujours insensiblement, de sorte que depuis la Naissance de J. C. les Etoiles paroissent avoir avancé de près d'un Signe, Et au bout de 25 mille ans la première Etoile du Bélier, après avoir passé par tous les Signes, reviendra à son premier Point.

La Terre, dans cette Hypothèse a deux mouvemens ; un Diurne et un Annuel. Le mouvement diurne est le Circuit et la Révolution que cette planète fait autour de son Axe, d'Occident en Orient dans l'espace de 24 Heures. Par là une même Partie de la Terre, se trouvant tantôt tournée vers le Soleil, et tantôt plongée dans les Ténèbres, les parties du Ciel qui se découvrent et qui se cachent successivement, paroissent tantôt se lever et tantôt se coucher. Le Mouvement Annuel est le chemin de la Terre dans le Zodiaque lorsque sa Surface roule par le Mouvement diurne autour de son Axe. Elle s'avance peu à peu, selon l'ordre des Signes, d'Occident en Orient, de même que le Centre d'une Boule qu'on fait rouler sur un plan avance suivant la longueur du plan, pendant que la Surface tourne autour du Centre de la Boule. De là vient que quand la Terre est entre le Soleil et un certain Signe, le Soleil cache alors le Signe opposé ; de sorte que si elle se trouve dans la Balance, le Soleil paroit être dans le Bélier. Si

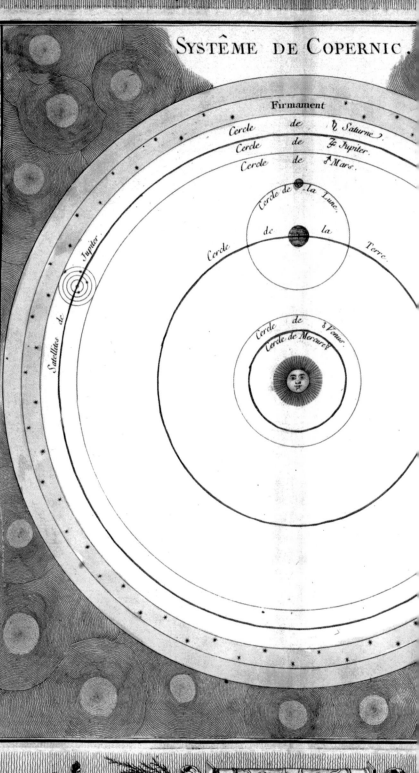

Firmament

Cercle de ♄ Saturne.
Cercle de ♃ Jupiter.
Cercle de ♂ Mars.
Cercle de la Lune.
Cercle de la Terre.
Cercle de ♀ Vénus.
Cercle de Mercure ☿.

Satellites de Jupiter.

GRAVITY

A Paris chez l'Auteur Rue St. Jacques, et chez Desnos son [...]

FROM HELIOCENTRISM TO BLACK HOLES

As far back as the 300s B.C., some people had argued in favor of a non-geocentric universe, but hardly anyone supported them. However, that didn't mean everyone was happy with the geocentric system. By A.D. 1252, Alfonso X, the new king of the Spanish kingdom of Castile and Leon, had ordered the development of a new set of mathematical tables to explain the movement of the planets. "If the good Lord had asked my advice at the time of the Creation," Alfonso reportedly said, "I would have suggested a simpler system of the universe."

Almost exactly three centuries later, Polish astronomer Nicolaus Copernicus (1473–1543) took up Alfonso's "suggestion" by developing a theory based on the heliocentric model. His theory involved much simpler mathematical calculations to account for planetary movement, and the book explaining it, *De Revolutionibus Orbum Coelestium* (*On the Revolutions of the Heavenly Spheres*), was finally printed as he lay dying. Although Copernicus's heliocentric ideas were widely circulated following his death, many people still held firm to the geocentric universe. The powerful Catholic Church supported the geocentric model of the universe, and Copernicus had no observational proof beyond his own calculations.

Johannes Kepler (1571–1630), a German mathematician and astronomer, took Copernicus's theory into the mainstream. After spending years making painstaking observations, Kepler devised three laws of planetary motion. The first states that planets orbit the sun following an elliptical path—a kind of oblong circle—rather than a circular one. Second, planets don't maintain a constant speed during their orbits. They speed up in the portion of the orbital path closest to the sun and slow down as they move farther away. For the third law, Kepler calculated how long it would take a planet to complete one full orbit, based on its average distance from the sun. Thus Mercury—nearest to the sun—completes a full orbit in 88 days, while Saturn—the farthest known at that time—needs 10,750 days (about 29 and a half years).

Around the same time that Kepler was developing his first two laws, Italian scientist Galileo Galilei (1564–1642) added more support for heliocentrism. In 1610, he used a newly invented telescope to discover several moons of Jupiter and realized they orbited that planet. That became the first hard evidence that not all heavenly bodies orbited Earth. Galileo believed that the way to understand how the world worked was through experimentation. For this reason, many people regard Galileo as the first true scientist. Some of his most famous experiments involved gravity. To test Aristotle's theory that heavier objects fell faster than lighter ones, for example, Galileo rolled balls of different weights down a grooved ramp. They all took the same amount of time to arrive at the bottom. Galileo concluded that all bodies fell toward Earth at the same rate regardless of their weight.

Such revelations paved the way for English physicist and mathematician Isaac Newton (1643–1727) to prove that the same basic laws ruled both earthly and heavenly forces. One day in 1666, Newton observed an apple falling from a tree. He realized that, no matter how tall the tree—or anything else—is, things always fall downward. People had begun using the word "gravity" just a few decades earlier to refer to the force that gives weight to earthly objects. Now Newton expanded the meaning to include the heavens. He called his idea the law of universal gravitation.

This law had three parts. One was that every object, whether a peanut or a planet, exerts a gravitational force over every other object—though only massive objects such as planets or stars exert a significant force. Second, the force between any two objects is directly proportional to multiplying their respective masses. Third, gravitational force varies with the **inverse square** of the distance between the two objects.

Newton couldn't measure the actual gravitational pull between two objects. That changed in 1798, when English scientist Henry Cavendish (1731–1810) suspended two

Galileo tried to convince officials of the telescope's importance

heavy metal balls about six feet (1.8 m) apart in a sealed room. He then placed a bar with two small metal weights between the balls. Using a telescope mounted in one of the walls, Cavendish could see and therefore measure the amount the bar was twisted due to the gravitational pull of the balls on the weights.

The next great advance in gravitational knowledge came from German-born physicist Albert Einstein (1879–1955). Einstein concluded that the speed of light (186,282 miles, or 299,792 km, per second) was absolute, or incapable of being compared with other things. If someone could travel at or near the speed of light, time and space would be different to this person than to someone else moving more slowly. This idea became known as the special theory of relativity. It brought Einstein into conflict with Newton, who had maintained that time and space were absolutes.

Playing the violin helped Einstein think through problems

The special theory of relativity didn't take gravity into account, so Einstein began working to solve this problem. A decade of painstaking mathematical calculations would follow. As he later said, "I occupy myself exclusively with the problem of gravitation.... Compared with this problem, the original theory of relativity is child's play." Early in 1916, Einstein finally published his general theory of relativity. In it, he combined space and time to form a four-dimensional **entity** known as spacetime. According to this concept, matter warps, or bends, spacetime, resulting in a gravitational pull.

f you roll a marble across a trampoline, it will follow a straight path to the other side. But if you place a bowling ball in the middle, the entire surface of the trampoline sags. The closer you get to the bowling ball, the more the sagging becomes evident. If you roll the marble again, it will curve down into the dip and circle the ball. The same thing happens in the solar system, Einstein said. The sun curves the spacetime that surrounds it. The planets simply follow that curvature because it is the shortest path. Even light is bent. Starlight seems to come from a slightly different origin than the actual position of the stars.

Another German physicist, Karl Schwarzschild (1873–1916), soon realized an important implication of the general theory of relativity. A star could collapse so much that all its matter would be packed into an incredibly tiny space. It would create such a deep dent in spacetime and have a gravitational pull so strong that nothing—not even light—could escape. Eventually, this phenomenon would be known as a black hole.

A new gravity-related mystery emerged in the early 1930s. Swiss astronomer Fritz Zwicky (1898–1974) discovered a large cluster of **galaxies** moving so rapidly that—based on their observable mass and therefore their gravitational pull on each other—it should break up. Because it didn't, Zwicky inferred that some kind of **dark matter**, with a mass far larger than what he could see, was holding it together.

No one followed up on Zwicky's observations until the late 1960s, when American astronomer Vera Rubin (1928–) examined stars at the outer edges of **spiral galaxies**. She expected that, like planets farther away from the sun, such stars would travel more slowly around the center of their galaxies. However, Rubin, along with fellow American astronomer Kent Ford (1931–), discovered that the stars at the perimeter were moving as quickly as the ones at the center. Since those stars didn't contain enough visible mass to produce the gravity needed to keep them all in orbit, Rubin and Ford concluded that they had proven the existence of Zwicky's dark matter. Today, dark matter remains one of the most important aspects of gravity research.

If all the energetic strings in the universe were visible, they could look like this

LOOKING DEEP INTO GRAVITY

Ever since Einstein added gravity to the special theory of relativity, physicists have been trying to develop a theory that unites the four fundamental forces—strong and weak nuclear forces, electromagnetism, and gravity—into one "super-force." The starting point more than a century ago was quantum theory. According to this theory, energy is carried in tiny packets called quanta. Some scientists believe that gravity's relative weakness might eventually result in its breakup into quanta. But the behavior of quanta cannot be predicted with absolute certainty, so we don't know how the other forces interact with it. Another model called the Grand Unified Theory, or GUT, was first proposed in 1974. It shows how, under conditions of especially high energy, the strong and weak nuclear forces and electromagnetism can be merged. But thus far, GUT can't fully account for gravity, either.

Some contemporary scientists, such as American theoretical physicist Brian Greene of Columbia University, believe a better possibility for unifying all the forces resides in string theory. According to this theory, which originated in the late 1960s, everything in the universe consists of incredibly tiny, constantly vibrating filaments of energy. These strings, which are hundreds of billions of times smaller than the nucleus of an atom, have just one dimension—length. In the same way that a single string on a musical instrument, such as a violin or a guitar, can produce many different tones, so these energetic strings are capable of producing particles such as **electrons** and protons. As Greene describes it, "the universe is like a grand cosmic symphony resonating with all the various notes these tiny vibrating strands of energy can play." If everything starts as electrons and protons on a string, then the fundamental forces could all ultimately be derived from different vibrations of the same basic string.

While Greene and others enthusiastically support string theory, it has one core problem. As American physicist Sheldon Lee Glashow of Boston University explains, string theory is "a kind of physics which is not yet testable; it does not make predictions that have anything to do with experiments that can be done in the laboratory or with observations that could be made in space or from telescopes." At this time, the theory rests entirely on mathematics, as no one has ever seen these strings, and as Glashow points out, no existing experiments can prove or disprove it.

Other areas of gravity research are easier to observe—but not so simple to test. Astronomers continue to investigate black holes, which they believe may contain vital information about how the universe began and how long ago that happened. They also seek more information about so-called dark matter. While little is still known about this mysterious material—despite the research of Rubin, Ford, and others—astronomers estimate that there is up to six times more dark matter than ordinary matter in the universe, and it therefore exerts a powerful gravitational attraction on stars and galaxies.

A particle detector called the AMS searches for dark matter in space

39

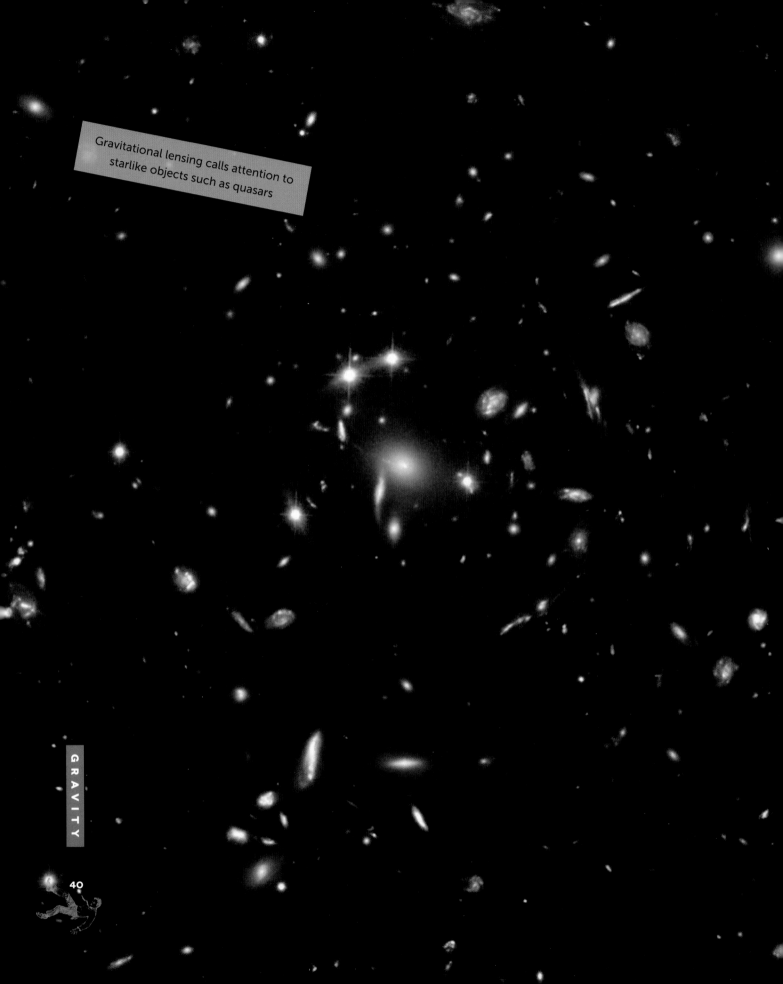

Gravitational lensing calls attention to starlike objects such as quasars

GRAVITATIONAL ASIDES

Riding Herd on a Satellite

film *Space Cowboys*, —played by Clint mes Garner, Tommy d Donald Sutherland— ly scheduled to become t astronauts. That ed, but years later, d upon when the ems on a mysterious e need repair. When e satellite, the men it carries several

nuclear missiles. Somehow they have to pilot it away from Earth toward the moon. Along the way, the film introduces some factual errors about gravity. One character says that a baseball would have to be hit only half the distance between Earth and the moon before the moon's gravity would take over. (The correct distance is actually nine-tenths of the way to the moon.) When a controller says the satellite has escaped Earth's

gravity en route to the moon, we know that couldn't be true, since the moon is still well within Earth's gravity, and the satellite hasn't even gone that far. A third misstep involves one of the characters landing on the moon with the satellite, which suggests he set it down without any damage. But in reality, the satellite would have hit the surface so hard— due to the moon's gravitational pull— that it would have been crushed.

Astronomers are eagerly awaiting construction of the Large Synoptic Survey Telescope (LSST) as a means of probing the mysteries of dark matter. The telescope, located in northern Chile and scheduled to begin operating in 2015, features an especially wide field of view and a very sensitive digital camera. The LSST will make use of a phenomenon called gravitational lensing, in which gravity bends light from distant objects in space around closer objects to create images visible to observers on Earth. It allows astronomers to probe billions of light years (the distance light travels in a year, which is nearly 6 trillion miles, or 9.7 trillion km) into space and detect possible concentrations of dark matter.

Far beneath the earth, another method of studying matter will be featured in South Dakota's Deep Underground Science and Engineering Laboratory (DUSEL). Scheduled for completion in 2016, it will be situated nearly a mile (1.6 km) down. The centerpiece of the dark matter lab will be a 660-pound (300 kg) tank filled with liquid xenon, a substance 3 times heavier than water, which researchers hope will trap dark matter particles.

LOOKING DEEP INTO GRAVITY

41

Other research relating to gravity has more immediate and practical applications. Because Earth is not a perfect sphere, certain locations experience small changes in gravity. Mountains project as much as six miles (9.6 km) into the atmosphere, and masses of ice, water, and other materials both on and under the earth's crust are constantly in motion. To chart the effects of these changes, in 1998 the National Aeronautics and Space Administration (NASA) and the German Aerospace Center (DLR) joined forces in a project named Gravity Recovery and Climate Experiment (GRACE). Four years later, GRACE launched 2 satellites (nicknamed Tom and Jerry), which orbit Earth at a distance of 137 miles (220.5 km) apart.

As the satellites pass over Earth's gravitational anomalies, sensitive instruments called accelerometers measure the distance between the two satellites with incredible accuracy. "This is like measuring the precise distance between a car in Los Angeles and one in San Diego [about 120 miles, or 193 km, apart] to within the thickness of a particle of smoke," says Dr. Michael Watkins, project scientist at NASA's Jet Propulsion Laboratory. A variation in distance between Tom and Jerry indicates a difference in gravitational pull. The program will continue at least through 2015 and reveal changes that can affect climate and other conditions on Earth.

What if humans were to explore places beyond Earth? They would need to take gravity with them to avoid the hazards of remaining weightless for long periods of time. Even for relatively short trips—such as the six-month journey to Mars—muscular weakening is an unacceptable side effect. The astronauts in deep space would be on their own and would need to be strong enough to deal with any possible emergencies.

NASA is experimenting with a vehicle that might prove useful for such journeys. It more closely resembles a space station than the sleek spacecraft portrayed in many

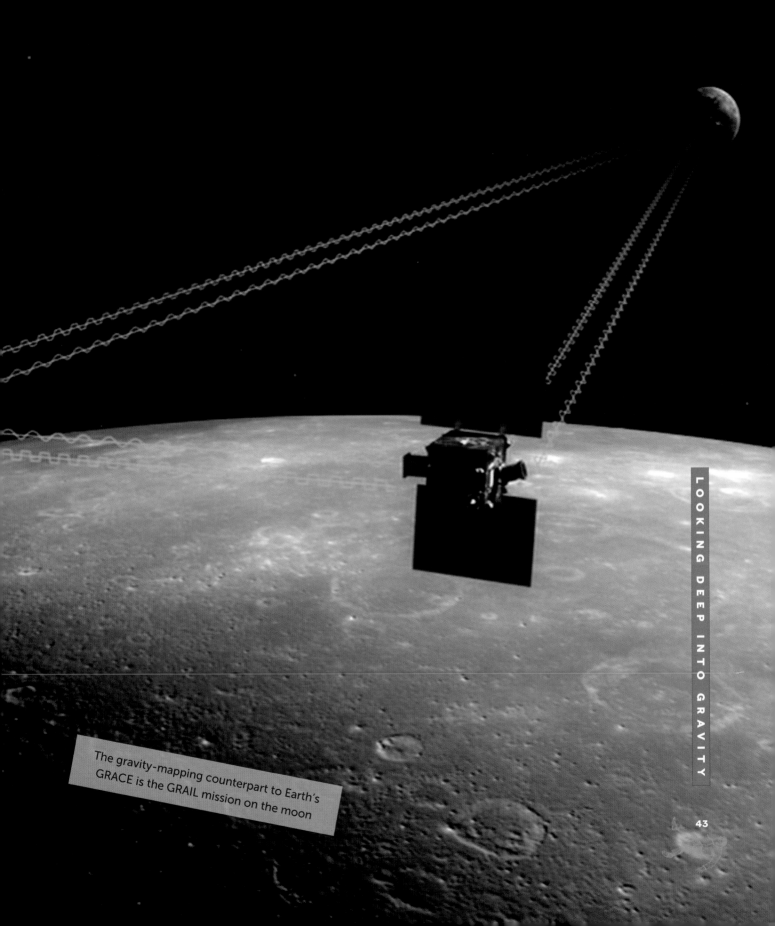

The gravity-mapping counterpart to Earth's GRACE is the GRAIL mission on the moon

Secrets of Weightlessness

One important organization working to uncover gravity's mysteries is NASA. With the International Space Station, NASA has an ideal laboratory in which it can conduct its research. The station's microgravity (weightless) environment allows astronauts to perform many types of experiments. Starting in 2010, astronauts began studying how seeds germinate in weightless conditions. They carefully monitored the seeds' growth and development, hoping to learn how plants respond to gravity and how the space station might become self-sustaining by growing its own food. Such research could improve agricultural practices on Earth, too. Apart from conducting experiments in space, NASA has found another way of achieving brief weightlessness. An airplane follows an up-and-down flight path that includes steep angles. During part of the flight, occupants in the padded body of the aircraft become weightless. At other times, gravity presses down on them with more than its normal force.

These flights, known as the NASA Reduced Gravity Research Program, are used to help train astronauts and enable college science and engineering students to "propose, design, fabricate, fly and evaluate a reduced gravity experiment of their choice," according to the program's Microgravity University Web site (http://microgravityuniversity.jsc.nasa.gov/). One recent experiment sought to reduce moisture inside the cabin of a spacecraft using a porous form of graphite.

science fiction films. The key element it features is a rapidly rotating machine called a centrifuge that would provide the artificial gravity needed for astronauts to exercise. A centrifuge produces the same effect as putting some water into a bucket, fastening the bucket to a rope, and then whirling it around your head as fast as you can. The force of the whirling motion keeps the water pressed against the inside of the bucket so it can't spill.

There's one mystery about gravity that researchers almost certainly won't be able to answer during our lifetimes: how gravity will influence the ultimate fate of the universe. Nearly all scientists believe that the universe is expanding, but they're not sure how long it will continue to do so. There seem to be three possible outcomes. The gravitational pull of all the matter in the universe may eventually halt this expansion, causing the universe to collapse. Or, at some point, the universe's expansion may surpass the pull of gravity, and the universe will continue expanding infinitely. Finally,

A zero-gravity facility in Ohio used for scientific research

the rate of expansion may decrease to the point where it is virtually equal to the pull of gravity. Then the universe would reach a state of **equilibrium**.

For most people, such long-term considerations aren't important. Newton's laws of gravity work just fine for them, explaining why they weigh what they do and even guiding astronauts to land on the moon. Yet scientists want more. They seek the answers to the deepest mysteries of gravity. While they don't have those answers yet, most believe that they will eventually discover them.

ENDNOTES

anomalies — things that are different from what is normal

archaeologists — people who study human history, primarily by excavating sites and examining the remains of what people left behind

artificial satellite — something placed in orbit around Earth or the moon to gather information or aid in communication

astronomers — people engaged in the scientific study of planets, stars, and other celestial phenomena

atom — the smallest part of an element with the chemical properties of that element

Babylonians — people of Babylon, a city-state in present-day Iraq that originated more than 4,000 years ago; for a time, Babylon was probably the world's largest city

command module — the part of the Apollo spacecraft that held the astronauts

dark matter — a type of matter that doesn't emit or reflect light but that exerts gravitational influence

density — the mass per unit volume measured in a substance

electrons — tiny, negatively charged particles that orbit the nucleus, or center, of an atom

elements — the basic parts from which all substances are formed

entity — something that exists and stands by itself

equilibrium — a state of balance achieved by forces canceling out each other

ether — the theoretical medium for transmitting light or heat

galaxies — systems of stars held together by mutual gravitational attraction and separated from similar systems by vast regions of space

geologists — people who study the history and physical structure of Earth, primarily by examining the rocks and minerals that compose it

germinate — to begin to sprout and put out shoots

graphite — a soft, dark form of carbon often used in pencils

International Space Station — the largest artificial satellite ever launched into Earth orbit; it was constructed between 1998 and 2011 and is usually staffed by a crew of six

inverse square — a physics law stating that an object's force of attraction is inversely proportional to the square of the distance from a point; expressed fractionally as one over the distance squared

lift — the interaction of airflow with speed over an aircraft's wings, creating lower pressure on top of the wings and causing the aircraft to rise

neutrons — tiny, uncharged particles found in the nucleus, or center, of an atom

orbit — the curved path that a celestial object takes around a larger celestial object

physicist — a person who studies matter and motion through space and time in an effort to discover the physical laws of the universe

porous — allowing the passage of gas or fluids

protons — tiny, positively charged particles found in the nucleus, or center, of an atom

radio waves — the longest waves on the electromagnetic spectrum; they can be used for communicating in radio, television, and cell phones

radioactive — giving off radiation, or electromagnetic energy, from an atom

science fiction — a type of fiction writing in which scientific principles or discoveries play an important role

spiral galaxies — galaxies structured like a spiral; arms with younger stars spiral outward from the center, where older stars are located

thrust — the force of a jet or rocket engine that propels it forward

WEB SITES

GRACE Games Center
http://www.csr.utexas.edu/grace/games/
Learn more about the Gravity Recovery and Climate Experiment with related games and activities.

Solar System Exploration: Your Weight in Space
http://solarsystem.nasa.gov/external/weight.cfm
Discover how much you would weigh at various points throughout the solar system.

SELECTED BIBLIOGRAPHY

Asimov, Isaac. *Isaac Asimov's Guide to Earth and Space.* New York: Random House, 1991.

Baker, Joanne. *50 Physics Ideas You Really Need to Know.* London: Quercus Publishing, 2007.

Bryson, Bill. *A Short History of Nearly Everything.* New York: Broadway Books, 2003.

Greene, Brian. *The Fabric of the Cosmos: Space, Time, and the Texture of Reality.* New York: Alfred A. Knopf, 2004.

Gribbin, John. *In Search of the Multiverse: Parallel Worlds, Hidden Dimensions, and the Ultimate Quest for the Frontiers of Reality.* Hoboken, N.J.: Wiley, 2010.

Hawking, Stephen, and Leonard Mlodinow. *A Briefer History of Time.* New York: Bantam Books, 2005.

Krysac, L. C., ed. *Gravitational, Electric and Magnetic Forces: An Anthology of Current Thought.* New York: Rosen, 2006.

Mazur, Joseph. *The Motion Paradox: The 2,500-Year-Old Puzzle behind All the Mysteries of Time and Space.* New York: Dutton, 2007.

INDEX